The Creek at the End of the Lawns

Other Books by Ira Joe Fisher

Remembering Rew, Bag-Tied-in-the-Middle Press, 2004
Some Holy Weight in the Village Air, Athanata Arts, Ltd., 2006
Some Holy Weight in the Village Air, NYQ Books, 2009
Songs from an Earlier Century, NYQ Books, 2009

The Creek at the End of the Lawns

Ira Joe Fisher

NY Books™

The New York Quarterly Foundation, Inc.
New York, New York

NYQ Books™ is an imprint of The New York Quarterly Foundation, Inc.

The New York Quarterly Foundation, Inc.
P. O. Box 2015
Old Chelsea Station
New York, NY 10113

www.nyqbooks.org

Gratitude is extended to the editors of the following journals in which some of these poems first appeared: "Age" and "Closing Time," *Entelechy International*; "Aftermath," *The New York Quarterly*.

First Edition

Set in New Baskerville

Layout and Design by Raymond P. Hammond
Cover Art by Patrick Mooney
Author Photo by Bill Snellings

Library of Congress Control Number: 2012948205

ISBN: 978-1-935520-65-8

The Creek at the End of the Lawns

for William D. Ford

Dear Billiam…
…They say you've died.
They say you're gone.
But if so how is it
that you still stand
upon my heart?
And smile.

Contents

The Creek at the End of the Lawns

Be Glad and Sing

(Psalm 67: 4)

The wind doesn't need
to spirit away your body
to spirit away your mind.

There need be
no lifting of form
to find a new place.

The sun will stab straight
into the darkness but only
as deep as you choose.

And when a sparrow sings
it brings morning, asking you
to wake and rise and meet it.

Dance

The maple leaf released
its hold on the topmost branch
and fell,
twirling down through fall,
down through the leaving light
twirling,
twirling
in a happy ballet in the air
to a soft stilling,
a quiet death
on the black street
paved with crepe.

At Heart

It rained today
As it had forty years ago
over Tachikawa.
I was new
in that eastern
garden of the globe,
young and strolling.
Under curved roofs,
green grass glowed
beside the flagstone path.
I was new there
and then.
That grass
and the sky
mixed a magic air
the color of graced light;
light more day
for being woven
wet of night,
wet of sea,
and of wraiths
who only had
my good
at heart.

An April Day

In the sun
a wind bothers
the boughs
of a pine
across the street.
It ripples
a canvas awning
as if thumbing
the pages
of an old book
so loved,
so read,
it sits open
and holy
like a bible
on the table.

There's no rent
in the sky,
no broken blue,
to tell
where the wind
slipped from.
It clears spring
for the sun
and the budding
to come.

Beginnings

You ask when I wrote my first poem?
1963. In Mister Felton's class.
Soon after Kennedy was shot.

Just after Essie moved with her family away,
Taking a piece of me she never returned.
Mister Felton, one Friday, said, "On Monday

We turn to poetry." Perry groaned.
Janie groaned. Robert laughed;
Then, groaned. And I thought (as I groaned),

No. Not poetry. That will be awful.
We'll need to read it. Bad enough.
But, you know he'll make us write, too.

And of what? I groaned, *of what?*
This was just when the Beatles crashed
Black and white into my life, our lives.

And Sophie cracked through the windshield
Of Louie's '50 Ford and gasped her last
At the end of a hundred foot fling

To the leafy grass beneath
The Governor's Street elm tree
That died with all the other elms

Around the time Nixon and Kissinger bombed
Cambodia. There were so many distractions.
Too many to allow the writing a poem.

But Mister Felton will have us write a poem.
We'll read a poem. We'll read poems.
And then, we're going to have to write one.

17

About…about something. But, what?
Write a poem when the world is so busy:
King marching to Selma and Hoover spying

In a flowered dress. Giff Carlyle setting fire
To his dry goods store for the money (and me
Thinking the hoses turned them into wet goods).

We're going to have to write a poem, I know
We are and Essie's gone to somewhere
In Ohio where now there could never

Be a poem. A poem needs drama.
Like a play by a Brit, like a novel
By that fellow who splattered his brains

All over a cabin wall out in Idaho.
On Monday, a unit on poetry
And Mister Felton will make us

Read poems. He'll make us write one.
And he did. And we did.
Mister Felton in his wool, three-button suit.

Black, cap-toe shoes…pointed and bent up
A little. Shirt white. Tie skinny.
He rode to work with Mister Randall.

They traded rides. One week Mister Felton
Drove his green Packard. Next week Mister Randall
Drove his gray Pontiac with a hood

Ornament of the Great Lakes chief
All silver and scowling and proud
And still looking for a Redcoat to hatchet.

A poem, I thought. *A poem,* I groaned.
About what? The snow is
Heaping up on the windowsill,

Drifting, mounding, sounding
With a whistling wind. Moaning
Like my thoughts of Essie

And umbrellas and held hands
And her abandoning Annville.
Mister Felton will have us open

Our book to the waterfowl page
Or the one with a certain slant of light
Or the woods, dark and deep.

The woods around Annville are like that.
But, there's no horse. And we go there
In pairs. To kiss, unbutton, and touch.

Lovely and deep are in the back seat.
And then the next morning
With sun and dust back home

Where the vacuum cleaner whines
And all I think about is last night,
Lovely and deep last night,

In a car by the woods
Where Indian burial grounds
Bulge the soft snow

And crackling leaves
And cracking trees
A sway in the wind and wishes.

And in the summer, Mister Felton splashed
His Packard into Chautauqua Lake
And never came up. Or back.

When, you ask, did a poem rise in me?
When I lost Kennedy and Essie…
…That's when I found words.

Ars Poetica

Rain
must be noted:
smell, thrum and chill
and fog waving at ending.
Rain must be noted.
The small bird:
swallow or finch.
Allow it to share your tree,
your land, your breathing
in the great green of summer.
The small bird must be noted.
See the leaves
seldom stilled,
see the leaves joyed and jostled
by wind in cool, blued afternoon
which must be kept
and held often and forever.
See the leaves
and see the leaf.
One and treasured
and living for that wind
until death on finished brown grass.
The sun behind the cloud
must be noted.
And the moon
and the thready edges
of that brief, mighty cloud
screaming quiet along the sky.
Note sun and moon and cloud
more living than a god.
Heed the haze dimming
the tops of cities
as if it were trying to hold
despair from rising.

Dimming haze must be noted.
A bridge, a river, banked bushes
washing the Allegany air
with the sigh of prayer.
Note these: bridge, river, bush.
Build what's remembered
on what's forgot
and sing of snow and night,
through winter's failing light.
A kiss on a porch
must be noted.
Even though it ends
in aching cold
frost-flecked and sparkled.
A kiss on a porch must be noted.
Load each day with the weight of a book
about jungles,
about wolves on the ice,
a book about the death of tramps.
Let the yellow glow
of the brown radio
bring distances to your eye and ear.
The steam from a pot of soup
must be noted
and how it began
throat-numbing cold
from a spring in pines
up the hill behind
the little house
where music and words
laid routes out and beyond,
seeking the grace of love.
The grace of love
must be noted.

And the joy of welcome.
Don't dither into bitterness
at waiting; feel the thanks
of welcome.
The thanks of welcome
must be noted.
And ink squiggles
on the creamy page,
let them paint colors
and scenes and voices:
a dark playground hiding
in woods just off the road,
a glass-tinked picnic,
and laughing at the coming of night,
the needles and leaves
of the leaving day
thinking sunlight is forever.
Picture some wakened wish
and hope on it.
Raise a tower
to see hills-away trees:
beeches, sumacs, firs.
Catch the staggering scent
of a country of cinnamon
and tents.
Cinnamon and tents must be noted.
Speak of stepping too light
to break the moonglow snow.
And lay a path of stones,
a path out of worry,
like an Asia wall.
A path of stones smoothed and waiting,
fished from the floor of the sea.
A path of stones must be noted.

Cringe at the hate
in a brother's red eyes,
a daughter's sleeping sadness,
an old woman who knew the brew
of no money
and homemade bread,
who knew how to break
dirt for corn,
how to break
dirt for graves.
Hoist your tower
one syllable at a time;
word upon word
upon word
and honor it
by holding a thing—
a fist, a lurch, a scraped chin,
grass-soft meadows and a dog—
holding a thing longer.
Each next minute
must be noted
like a host at church,
like a glowing song from a far place,
a tower of thoughts,
of words of what must be noted:
torn sneakers,
a rope on a beam in a barn,
a charred brick factory,
crayfish,
creeks,
a hammock in the silence
of maples,
a stuttering lake
and how a cow stood

by a fence flicking flies
with her tail.
Mountains and long miles,
long miles, long miles away.
These and goodbyes
must be noted.

Word Worry

The squat deliveryman frowns, bending
beneath the box of commerce he bears
into the café where I sit.

Or is the box lumped with waiting spirits
eager to mist and twist
and knock things down?

How has he come to these tasks
of packing a truck and driving a route
and lifting?

The hair on his arms floats
over a blue tattoo like a gypsy curtain
dimming the light within.

How am I blessed to sit and sip and read
hefty words, lifting them
to touch the morning sun?

Will my words work? Will they *lift*?
Or hold heavy and rooted
To the page?

Or will a robin-riled breeze
toss them up, up to leaves and fuzzy buds…
And cause the deliveryman to sneeze?

Disguise

I invited the breeze
by opening the door,
and in it came
from a roof-high moon
that glowed a season closer
in summer-thick air.
It smelled of a ghost
from the forest
or bent hay
or a woman mistaken
for a queen.
I felt a pang
for the lowering moon,
and wondered
if it would ever rise again.

Apples and Salt

Harleigh was meticulous in two things:
folding *The Annville Hub* at the middle

(then raking its crease on the table edge)
and he always sprinkled apples with salt.

The rest of life slogged wrinkled and sooty.
Books piled in the sagging room where he slept.

They drooped in precarious stacks. The books
seemed to glow so he could read them, read them

even in dark. The room smelled of apples;
strong in fall: macintoshes, northern spies.

A salt shaker kept guard on the night stand,
so he could take his apple with a grain.

The newspaper rippled as Harleigh chewed;
its oozing juice bite as cold as metal.

If you ever thought of him, you would think
of apples and salt; how he never looked

at you when he spoke about such things as
bootlegging out of Canada. He'd look

down at the worn thread in the once-blue rug
while he picked at red skin around his nails.

Some of the stories cut a smile across
his grayed face, stories haunted of hellions

snubbing the law. Of smuggling whiskey
over the Peace Bridge into Buffalo;

whiskey in hot water bottles belted
to his stomach, buttoned under his shirt.

But now back in Annville his life was slowed
like the oil from a crank shaft in winter.

He worked ten hour days, six days a week,
standing, aching in a greasy, dank pit

under a rich somebody's sedan. He
tuned up the town from down in a cement hole.

He'd climb out at twelve; to pull an apple
from his gray lunch bucket and two thick white

slices of home-baked bread. He'd pour a cup
of crow-black coffee brewed the night before.

Doc Busch insisted only Harleigh keep
his yellow Buick murmuring and clean,

rotate the whitewalls and polish the chrome
and gently scrape summer bugs from the grill.

Doc Busch wanted the car in good order
for runs to the hospital or dirt road

rides with a woman who wasn't Missus
Busch. Doc liked Harleigh. Harleigh didn't care.

Nestor, his boss, always paid him in cash
each Friday night. Harleigh'd buy a fish fry

that they wrapped in a newspaper over
at the Red Mill, to take home for supper.

He'd make sure to have a glass of something,
followed by another. And another.

So a numbing seeped into coveralled
Harleigh. He'd lie back on his bed and spin

with the world to sleep. Deep, dark, sleep. In air
like dark oiled air in a mechanic's pit;

dreams of dead dogs and the smell of loaded
shotguns. And the taste of apples and salt.

Hale Farm

In the speeding, fading century
you're beside the sun-caught corn,
and then the house beside the barn
and you slow. You slow as if
you're taking off your hat in church.
House and the barn bear that spirit.
House and barn and fields are holy.
The clapboards sit as flat
and straight as the day
they were pegged into place
two centuries ago. Paint hangs
like vestments. The mailbox says *Hale.*
The black earth speaks of flowers
and hay and corn and oats and peas
and potatoes and beans. The black earth
opens for the peonies climbing
the trellis beside the porch
against the kitchen where the food
was served to the haying hands.
You slow and see the dung hill
grown to grass, the barn doors
shut, locked. Farmer Hale even mowed
between house and road.
After twice-a-day milking,
after pitching bales down from the mow,
after climbing the silo,
after disking, raking, carting the milk;
after squinting at the sky,
smelling for rain, after biting
the green, sugary stem of the grass
from the meadow by the creek;
after unloading the stone boat
(and making a home for snakes),
after brushing and bedding the horses

and walking work-weary
over the dust-powder drive
to the house under the pines,
Farmer Hale even mowed
between his house and the road.

Glance

My headlights bathe a vine
as I scratch around a dusty corner.
Autumn has drained
the leaves yellow.
In this too-quick turn
in the too-quick night
the vine hangs like the tentacle
of a dryly dying octopus
thirty sad miles from the sea.

The Current War

Is the beautiful poet silenced?
Does the curer of cancer
Lie in her grave?
Is the sunny-haired joker's
Laughter stopped, stunted, done?
What trees have blown their shade
To smoke?
Are the scampers
of squirrels cut
short of making smiles?
Hitlered, Stalined, Bushed.
We speak, we speak of the *current* war.
But there's always war
To weave dread in us
Or amuse the bastards
Who'll never have to fight it.

Apostrophe to Grass and the Place He Chose

On the muddy March slope
you crumble the earth
with your determined green growth.
You spear, you frond, you blade, you grass.
April steals brown winter
and sleight-of-hand budding
grows leafy and damp.
You reach, you rise, you grow, you seek,
seek the sun, riding its east-to-west dome;
you take the gild into your delicate stalk
of sugar and strength and wind-bend
to become June field, to become July hay,
to become crop, to become food
to sit in the dark barn mow
where Eben Tolley will stand
one August morning
with a pheasant gun his grandfather gave him.
Where he'll blast the chaff from the rafters
as the shot rips the side of his head
to a sticky red seeping on the hay
drying and cooling and waiting
for Thursday to find him
there on you, the just-cut hay,
you that grew in the field
that came to the barn
to feed the cows.
Cows, who now
will be sold
or butchered
to pay
for
things.

Who Better

Who better
to become an angel
of peace
than the ghost
of a soldier
sent into the white
heat
of war?

Who better
to enter foul, insane
hatred
and understand
the horror
and the need
to do away
with it?

C. O.

Mister Government, do you still
hold a fading thought
that war
that killing
that sending them to fight
is a sin?
Oh, you still plan war,
you start war, you rage.
You still fight.
You still kill.
But do you hold a thought,
a fading thought
that it is a sin?
I only ask
because you still call
war's objector
conscientious.

Bereavement

Beside the road,
just above the forest floor,
as I slipped south
like a Carolina pelican,
I saw a broken tree.
It drew a new angle
among its neighbor pines.
They were scrubbed straight
under a sky of boughs,
over the sandy earth.
Even the day
was eyes-down dark
among the standing trunks.
A family
at the grave
grieving to learn it was
one less in number.

Games

Look, look where the chimney smoke
Wisps up from chipped brick upon
The roof of the weary wood
Cottage leaning on the grass.

All the small houses show gray
Splintering the paint on boards
Buzzed out of the woods to sing
In the sawmill dirt roads down

Yellowed years from this sunken,
Shrunken village still small as
Its birth before brotherly war,
Ungrown and halted with folk

Who breathe the hilly shadows,
Who fight clawed fears with spirits.
Who sag from the jobs and glooms
That own them here and bubble

A strange, strange thirst to keep them
From smiling at their children
Who play in the creek with thin
Dogs untethered, cats unhoused.

Deer tremble in the woods,
They cringe at hanging blood-dead
On the creaking tavern porch
Smelling of whiskey and grease.

Rifles and drink fuel the men
And fool the women silent.
Like the Ellicottville Road
And that to Salamanca

They split, speed apart, away
From a small marrying hope
That started in rented suits,
Started the unraveling

Of not holding hearts, of eyes
Aimed down and beyond and red.
All that is left of this game
Are ragged sons and lost girls

Who ache too young with worry,
Who wish the radio could
Lift them in upon a song,
Upon a laugh, hiding grief.

There is a boy spinning thoughts
Of swimming and kick-the-can
In the sacred summer air
Beneath the shouldering hills

Who breathes the hilly shadows
And conjures his laughing games:
Climbing doomed elms, splashing creeks,
Sweating his bike up Mill Street,

Clover-green baseball, capture
The flag and later under
The haze of summer and lust
Of unbuttoning buttons

And pulling aside lacy
Confinements to throbbing warmth,
Hands holding and hands moulding
The cloud-downed skin of young girls.

These are the games of a boy
In a town whose souls are sunk
Into shadows seeping down
From the silent, wooded hills.

The Creek at the End of the Lawns

Herewith a tale of love and wondering.
A time when leaves stir the wind to confer
Its magic and for grass to light the sun.
Herewith a telling of years-apart souls,
A boy and a ghost who have things to ask.
And they meet in a village—in Annville
Whose life is light and shadows (happiness
And laughing once bubbled up from houses
Between peonies and under maples
Under looming oaks and blued, stirring firs).
Around the great war of the century
(Which saw lightning blaze more wars) fragmented,
Splintered an errant bolt that hit Annville
And blessed some of the village's quiet
Folk with a blued, stirring sense, a knowing
About magic things benighted people
Cannot know. Or see. Or do. Darkly strange.
Oh, still there was summered sun and winter
Loping snowed out of the colored and leaf-
Smokey autumn, but night took hold of souls,
Of the souls in the village, and lightning
Wove a weaving to the strings of a bridge
Between those hearts and those souls, as I say,
Of chosen villagers to understand
More deeply mysteries before the great
Didactic death. And then even greater
Secrets and fretted puzzlings of life long…
Or lopped short that before would cause the heads
To shake, to purse the lips of villagers
Who could not grasp such knowing as it rose
And vapored and waved and wisped soft away
Like the pollen riding the goldenrod
Little boys used to make their swords and forts
And girls braided to fashion green cradles

To hold babies who saw with plastic eyes
And the pollen yellowed the air with its
Rising and leaving and sparkling like dreams.
This town, this Annville, named by a blacksmith
Who saw life there as cold and hard and sparked
By angers that grew in the very dust
Of the two-centuries-ago roads and streets,
Angers that could not stay buried beneath
Boards, then bricks, then asphalt as the village
Centuried on and boys aged to steal beer
And the girls mothered babies with *real* eyes.
A boy and a ghost meet. How, you ask? How?
By the magic of leaves stirring the wind,
By the magic of grass blazing the sun.
The boy hikes from his fellows to follow
Silence into the hills above Annville
And he learns there will never be silence,
Learns there will never be silent silence.
He feels the itch of the paper that rests
Upon his scarred desk or reddish-gray shale,
Upon moss that pillows hillsides; all this
Brings him words riding on air, upon scents
Burrowing up from dark loam where before
Only corn, cabbages, and potatoes
Burrowed and sprouted for tables, not dreams.
The boy sensed stories *in* the dark, hairy
Earth. *From* that earth where all things fall in fall
(*Calendar* fall of leaves and crops cutting
Their cords for good, for goods. Or *mortal* fall,
That grave, peopled season of leaving all
Behind). The boy and pen found tales sprouting
In his sprouting soul. Stories joined his hopes
For love and leaving Annville for the glow
Of a spinning, wheeling, beckoning world

That looked to be looking at the young boy.
The world *looked* at the boy, Annville *spoke*.
And what it said inked his pen for scratching
That paper itch to tell the town's stories.
The night woods became a good ghostly place.
Like books freed of their covers, releasing
Imprisoned words and stumped sounds
And songs breathed by the heart out of the lungs
Into people musicked to a cool weft
That a blessed visitor—a boy—could hear
And shudder and guide his pen to paper.
The night woods became a good ghostly place.
Like a clock in a tavern, the night woods
Always tampered with time. But while taverns
Encouraged their dim clocks to tick ahead
The woods ordered their clocks to look and tick
Behind and drag time back, back, back with it.
A place where old folks are always old folks
And a place where the young are always young.
In the night woods time doesn't age, nor do
Minutes ever decay. Night commands it.
The tree-dark air in the night forest smelled
Of a curious pleasure, that leads to
A contentment or a wond'ring story
Of what each new, next moment might offer
Of love or menace. Away from sidewalks,
Ballfields, heaving streets and the lamps above
Those streets and kissing on the town porches.
Into the good, ghostly woods above town
Breathed a thick, humid, shadowed lust of air.
The boy—with aching head, smarting eyes—
Learns there will never be earthly silence
Because all we've spoken, all we've sung lives,
Lives in the wrinkling, mottled, dew-damp air

44

And zooms off in speech and song forever.
The boy gets a gift from the Annville hills.
It's all the wisdom and all the gossip
Soaked into valley vines and heaving hay.
He learns of love and breathing 'neath the veil
Of years. A thing few mortals ever learn:
That love, veiled upon the hills, is still love.
It is still there, he learns, it is still love.
So the boy writes these Annville lessons down.
And the very ink of those words vibrates
Into streams from the brittled, yellowing
Paper. And those streams summon a spirit,
A ghost who sees life from inside a tree,
From the breast of a bird, from a deep creek.
A ghost can go where he wills. Anywhere
From the treed hills and from the hilly trees
Ghosting over brick houses, clapboard shacks,
Ghosting through the froth and freeze of winter,
Weaving in the wetted breaths of strangers
And the ones who loved and grieved his dying
Through the veil hazy and undulating,
A veil the color of spring snow slowly
Steaming and sculpting spring into hissing
Full-blown summer: wig'ling creeks, mossy banks.
Through the heaving, needing lawns of the town
Awash with rose bushes, silky cornstalk,
The fondling and kissing on a boy's mind.
The sky is washed with a latter-day black.
Inky trees lean over the village street.
A pale and pooling moon lights these two souls:
A young man with shirttails out and a ghost
In clothes the color of this night above
The Annville hills. This ghost is called Alfred.
The young man is Finch. How is it these two

Meet in soft summer, on the deep green earth
To speak, to grieve, to argue of hidden
Things the young and living boy oddly knows?
Finch ought to have been thrilling to baseball
On the radio, in his darkened room
In the house his father raised before death
Left questions scattered in his mind like drek
At a September fairgrounds. So he wrote
About what he saw, about who he knew.
And with each scratch of the pen, the scratching
Of the paper's itch, an itch of his own
Is met to speak of what he sees, what he
Feels of a knowing growing ever close.
Only a mortal few ever enter
The dark where ghosts spin and hover and wait
To speak, to teach, to reach such visitors.
Alfred and Finch have met before this night
In other nights where their questions sparkled
Like reluctant lightning—after a strike—
Unwilling, unprompted to die to dark.
While understanding that it is the night,
The living and breathing, sentient night
Who decides gatherings and writes the roles
Of characters in this nocturnal play
And its lightning and its searching wisdom.
And it was a forest, a night, a ghost
That drew the boy without fear, without dread
To find a knowing…about a village,
Its people and the suspension of love.
Each time they met, and talk inflicted pain,
Finch worried they'd not meet again, so he
Had pretended to be the decider.

"What gives you leave to tell town tales?" the ghost
Challenges Finch. Because he summoned Finch.

To ink on paper the tales of the town.
The night woods became a good, ghostly place.

"Leave?" Finch tries to be light, "I took my leave
Of you." In the dark, Finch tries to be light.

Lines deepen on Alfred's forehead. "Your glance
Won't work with me, won't work at all. I am
All the wraiths hovering smoke-like over
Annville. Noticing." The moon, behind trees,
Flutters from shadows in the humid air.

And here Finch tries leaning back, casual.
"We both know what we both know. About drink
About betraying; all about being."
"Don't," the ghost of the village snarls, "don't sneer.
You were born of us; seasoned four seasons
Each year. You know of snow, the smell of smoke
And leaves and the burn of ball-bat blisters.
D'you forget I sensed you on girls' porches,
Your mouth open and your hands up to things?"

"Wait," Finch reddens, "I was a boy, with hopes
Plotting a fast path out of your thick air.
I sipped a sip at your table, but it
Was low and dusted with something death-like."

Alfred ripples like water in the wind.
"Oh, spare me your head-down, imagined hurt.
If we two are to weave a common thought,
If we will ever join before your grave,
Then, let us...*you*...tell of the village, truth."

Finch is a versifier, bard, a scop.
And Alfred has opened the night forest

47

For the boy to enter, to learn. To tell.
Learn he has, but not yet all he must learn.
Finch has peered into the past and seen scenes
That live in that room called "a soul," that live
Piled beside the piled years and all waiting
For a fine noticing of who was then;
And what was said and thought and done and brought
Into this leafy place that Finch calls "now."
The modern, the new, the current...the now
Diff'rent speeds, sounds, and sights like the ironed
Flat thunder of a passing jet. Finch speaks:

"Each street breathed beneath trees—maple and elm
And they were what I wrote of when I wrote
Of town. The trees and the flowers and lawns
And of the creek at the end of the lawns
And how they powdered the air with something
Soft and green. I spoke of that when I spoke."
Something far, something warm draws Finch's eyes.

"You also would tell of sawdust and beer,
A wood-stove in the shack at the skating
Rink, remember? And how the fallen leaves
Of fall smoldered and smarted your eyes. You
Wrote of that," Alfred spits a smokey spit.

"Ah, there were many smells, I must admit:
Apples, oil, beered air from the bars, diner
Burgers and cream soda, sunny fur on
A beagle's back, swaying hay, cut and forked
On old wagons, beans trucked on trucks through town.
I did smell them and the smells had to work
On my mood, on what of my town I knew."

The ghost looked back from some top of a hill.

48

"But people? What have you said about folks?"

"Why don't you ask what I've thought about folks?"

"Talk. Thought. When you're a smoky ghost, it's all
The same. Talk, thought and pulling down, slowing
To a stop…" Alfred pockets his gray hands.

"Death, you mean."

"There you go, knowing more than time, than ghosts;
Knowing a thing that can't be known. You're no
Different, you simply, sadly, think you are.
You smell the gray wet wool of tears."
"Or smell *of* them…"

"Oh, yes, yes. You do smell of them. Of tears.
You're not the only one. You are alone
But you're not the…only one. I'll tell you
Of a woman name of Amis. She lived
On Erie Street. Made Erie Street pretty
With flowers planted from porch to sidewalk;
With her eyes, her smile, her form and her love
For Astin." Alfred rubs his veiny hands.

"Astin Amis? Wasn't her name Laura?
I think I knew them."

"You knew him. An old man. But Laura died
a while before you were born. And Astin
Worked in the grocery. You knew him there.
Small store—three aisles piled to the tin ceiling—
Over on the corner of Main," the ghost
Points wearily. "'Neath the Masonic Hall."

"I can still hear the click of the pool balls."

"There's sure a memory a boy would have!
Pool balls clicking in the Masonic Hall!"

Finch tugs his ear. "What do *you* remember?"

"Why, everything! Snow whiskering the town.
Deep enough so stores'd shovel a tunnel
From the curb to the door. Cold enough, too.
I'd trudge all through the dark village winter."
It is here Alfred smiles a closed-lip smile
"But don't believe a ghost who claims to trudge.
Travel is no trudge. It's a rippled slip,
A sigh. Some hold the faith that winter's cold
Is meant to boil the rot out of the soul,
The spirit of folks you like to call bad."

"I'm in no shape to call anyone bad."

"No one is. In shape to do that, I mean.
But you do. Everyone does. No excuse,
Just a fact. Boil the rot out of the soul.
That's what the cold does, I believe, I feel."

"True?" Tossing his head, Finch leans toward the ghost.

"It's what I feel! And the wind is telling
Us, us ghosts, us holding-all, telling us
That what happened was supposed to happen;
That people are right where they're meant to be."
Alfred's cave-eyes rise above the boy's head.
"The dead I'm talking about, with the rot
Boiling out of their souls."

"Did Laura Amis have rot in her soul?"

"No. She lay abed in the hospital
After her baby died. Her baby lived
Only days. Laura suffered a fever,
Could hardly raise her arms. Her sweet daughter
Had no chance. Just a start. And then an end."

"Sick mother, sick child." Finch regards the ground.

"And the little girl died. In Laura's arms.
At her breast," Alfred looks down, too. "Wasted."

"Did they see it coming?"

"They only saw life going. The babe's. Theirs.
They had seen life shining when they were young.
Astin worked a farm. Holsteins on a hill.
From its tree-ringed meadow-top, Astin looked
Down to the schoolhouse where his Laura taught.
They'd met at a grange dance and love lifted
Them both above the slick chaf-dusty floor…
And they never came down. Laura hated
Farms and Astin hated farming, so he
Sold the cows and house and barn and he bought
The little cottage on Erie Street. He
Painted it green with darker green shutters
And he took a clerkship in the three-aisled
Grocery. He didn't miss the hill-farm
(Oh, just a sweet-eyed cow or three). Astin
Was with Laura. She taught until she knew
Their baby was coming, then retreated
To the porch, to rock in a chair and smile
At her flowers blossoming to the walk.
Then…it all went sad."

Finch sunk and he sighed, "The baby girl died."

"Laura lay abed in the hospital
List'ning to the bells from the old stone church.
The bells of her own baby's funeral."

"God."

"I wonder."
"You? You wonder about God? *You* wonder?"

"Yes. I wonder still as I sigh and slip
Through town. There is no all-known, all-knowing."

Finch thrusts out his chin, "I'd think you would know."

"Well, such thinking is why you're still alive;
Starting and young and why you lowly know.'"

"What. Am I stupid? You think I'm stupid?"

"Don't underline it. But listen. Quiet
Yourself and hear the wind old in the trees.
Know the only music is what you call
'The minor key.' Always sung in sorrow.
Sad and grieving. Leaving dust on your tongue,
Thistles stabbing you deep in your belly.
So, don't underline your stupidity,
But wisp away from it. Hear the wind old
In the trees."

"Do *you* hear it? Do *you* hear the wind old?"

"Ah, in a most ghost-like way, you wonder?
Rising in fog from the creek at the end

Of the lawns? From the cutlery's chipped bricks?
The clock click in the dark diner at night?
Or how bats whiffle through the court house air
In the dome o'er the elms? Do *I* hear it?
You would have me say secrets; tell my truths."

"I would." Finch looks eager here. On his toes.
Like waiting to dart onto a ballfield.
"You want me to say my secrets, do you?
You want me to tell of dogs needling
Their toenails on the sidewalk and sniffing
The air as we sniffed the air: for some small
Adventure. You want me to tell of cars:
Willys and Packards and Studebakers
They don't make anymore. There were workers
And teachers and bartenders and barflies
And waitresses and dairymen and clerks.
Shall I tell about fish fries and burgers,
Ginger ale, chilled milk, stolen, bitter beer?
O, how our Annville glowed in the colors
Of autumn, how it smelled of Christmas firs
And winter coloring its shadows blue.
How spring was more a hope than a season.
A hope, a prayer prayed to melt the slow snow
And green the brown to green. Then comes summer.
Summer. All hazed and baseballed and shaded
By the ghosts-of-grandfathers 'neath the trees.
Let me tell you what I prayed to the wind:
Rush the corner room with violin sighs.
Stitch the sky with trees, O wind, tremble, flow.
Turn my roof from roof to knife and bear ghosts
To dance your sounds a-swirling, curling down.
Stroke so high that the climbing bird is kin
To the bending grass, to the nodding branch.

Call me, wind, in dark or day, chill and rain.
Call me, wind, call me true, I'll soon be you."

Finch is pulled to these woods by a silent
Sense in his chest, by a breath behind his
Eyes, by a knowing there is more to learn
Of the dark, of the night, under a moon
Or under no moon with stars a-tumble
At sky-play and not caring who sees them
Or those who choose to sleep. For this questing
Boy, these woods and these talks with a sad ghost
Are not adventures. They are a deep need.
And he knows what Alfred means in praying
To the wind. He knows what the wind prayer means.
Finch just presses his lips hard together
And peers through the wraith, the shade before him
As though he sees the far hill all lighted
In the night and he wants, again, to know.
"Yes," is all he says, still looking away.

"You seek secrets from me? Assurances?
I musn't. But I can speak of regret.
I worked days with grease on my hands, my arms.
I sweated in denim and steel-toed shoes.
I hammered starred sparks up from an anvil,
Burning holes in my undershirt, scarring
My chest and neck. I thought about my son.
My youngest. He came after I wearied."
Alfred runs his vein-ey hands through his hair.
"The boy waited nights for a game of catch.
That big mitt on his skinny, sunburned arm.
I tried...oh twice. And never tried again.
Too damned tired, is what I thought. Too damned tired
Is what I was—of work—work six damned days.

I splashed a splash of water in my face,
Downed a jelly glass of port 'fore supper."

"Your boy wanted *you* and you wanted wine."

It is here ghostly Alfred seems to breathe
And look away. "In one of those lives...yes."

"*One* of those lives? You mean you've lived before?"

"Now, don't go prying. You have to be kept
From knowing, from certains. That's why folks don't...
Why folks don't visit all the world's places.
Our *thoughts* are better than their *facts*. The grass
And pebbles. How the wind steals the vapor
From a fountain as it falls and then throws
It at the pastor's hat or mayor's wife..."

"Or how I just might understand." Finch pouts.

"Understand. Hmph! You talk too much. You *do*."

New moonlight hallows the air. And it smells
Of leaves and rain and the blue glow of night.
Rilling, the creek at the end of the lawns
Grows old and wise in its rush. In its rush
Through town it seems to the boy to always
Glance back to learn if he will stay. Or flee.
The creek, like the night and the woods knows things.
The creek, like mist and susurating leaves
Knows things. About a boy, ghosts and a girl;
What's hope-hung in their hearts. What's fear-hung,
too. And now our creek, on its skirting current
Lifts a feathered white vapor to the ghost

Slumped and wearied who looks away from Finch
And back, takes a deep, filling breath, and asks,
"Why do you never talk about Essie?"

"It's enough to simply think about her."

"*Is* it? Is it enough? To simply *think*
About her? And the notes you wrote? The notes
You read?" If Alfred taunts, he also smiles.
"Ah, my boy, you still hum with your green needs
For sweet Essie who reigns upon your mind
Smiling, dimming but never lost or gone.
Finch, our days are about choosing, you know?
All about choosing. Even when we think
We're tossed from here to heaven and back down.
And when that choosing looms in coming years,
When you lie in loony night…tense, troubled,
Re-living, re-hurting, regretting times
Tipped over and back, tipped over and missed,
I say *you* know of ghosts more ghost than I.
Ghosts who rise, look away from your hurt heart,
Ghosts who shun the heated meeting of eyes
Young, unclouded and glistened to a smile.
But, a choosing comes and dimming begins.
Love freezes. And all that grows is regret.
Do you know our days are about choosing?"

"Essie knows. Essie knows about choosing
And staying. And keeping the wider world
Beyond her door and lamp. Beyond her life.
O, I loved…*love* Essie. I have two dreams:
The world. And a girl. Essie. I will leave
And *she* will stay. She is a town away.
But when I leave the towns will multiply
And the miles like the years will pile higher

So that only remembering will make
The dark sparkle. And a kiss on the porch
Will mist from kiss to memory...to pang."

"And what did Essie say to you, my boy?"

"She said, 'You must go, Finch. Go and forget.
The world is calling to *you*, not to *me*.
I cannot leave these little village hills.
In that calling world, you hear adventure.
I hear fear, worry at what I don't know.
The hillsides around us are never blue.
Have you noticed? Noticed they're never blue?
Even in rain or winter...when the trees
Lay gray across the patient snow. And they're
Not mountains. They're hills and the Annville hills
Sit close and quiet...never far enough
Away to be blue. Finch, I can not leave
Dandelions and backyards and willows
And sweet wild strawberries in the meadow,
Pines along the drive or red wintergreen
In the dewed sod and grass beside the creek.'"

The recalling stabs the recoiling boy.

"'I saw the stabbing in your eyes, my Finch.
And how I wished you would say you would stay;
But that was brief and selfish from my proud
And timorously leaf-like heart. I love...'"

"Yes? Yes? O, say it, Essie, O, say it!"

"'I can not. I must not. For to say it
Would, I do fear, keep you from each new, next
Moment and to make of love a menace

When the fire of our desire turns gray like
The naked trees on the wintering hills.'"

"O, Essie, come with me and we'll find hills
And little valleys, the songs of bright bands,
The tunes of birds and traffic, the music
Of each new, next moment that we can pile
And seal with sun and love and our knowing
What we *sense* is true. What we *know* is true."

"So you know our days are about choosing."

"Will I know, will I, Alfred? Will I know?
Oh, speak of ghostly things! Tell of that house
Near the swamp, that house with a ragg'ed flag
I saw through the dirty parlor window.
Please speak of mossy banks on wiggling creeks
Or the rising, falling, crumbling sidewalks
Weaving along the heaving streets and yards
Behind the houses, under the street lamps.
Don't speak of kissing, but speak of leaves.
Do speak of ballfields and folk songs and barns...
With their flitting swallows, morning-gloried
Robins giving a gift of bird-beauty
To village and farm. Speak of how barbed wire
Counted all the cows and mapped their mooing
Out of the paths of bicycling boys
Lusting about for bicycling girls
As June and July baked hedges and hay
In the humid and fragrant lust of air."

"But not of Essie? There's a vexing there,
Isn't there? You don't want to talk of that.
Of her." The ghost turns gentle. The smile leaves.

"Stop," Finch sighs, sinks, begs.

"Walking head-to-head beneath her mother's
Old black umbrella. Holding hands; smelling

The rain and puddles upon the sidewalk,
Along Fair Oak Street. A restaurant dinner
And you forgot to pay. You two walked out
Holding hands, holding hearts, holding…breathing."

And Finch's voice coarsens, "Years gone. Years gone."

"To a wispy one as I, years are breaths;
They're brief and piled, piled, piled. And piling still.
To a wispy one, twenty years ago
Is the just-breathed breath, hanging in the creek-
Odored air."

"Stop being wise. Stop teaching. Or posing."

"I don't *pose*! And don't you dare *say* I do!"

"I shouldn't think that you would let something
A someone like me would say get under
Your skin. That is if you had any skin."

"How do you dare rudeness? Dare such rudeness
To me, a spirit you don't understand?
How do you trust that I can be trusted?
That I won't deal you some *thing* you'll regret?"

"Oh, I didn't mean to be rude. Truly.
I only meant to be funny. A ghost
Can't laugh?" It is here the ghost relaxes.

"Yes. Can one pine for a weeping willow?
Strange that life always ends in the mourning.
I can laugh at how the sagging tavern
Stairs creak and sigh at each thirsty footstep.
I can laugh at eggs splattered on the wall
Of the school and on the math teacher's house."

"England has no national anthem. True.
'God Save the Queen' resounds through the kingdom
Diminishing though it is. But England?
No national anthem just for itself.
But why would they need one? They don't even
Play baseball over there."

"Hell! I can find it funny that the bank
President spends three afternoons a week
Parked in his car with Fern, the hat store clerk;
Parked 'neath the oaks on the road beyond town.
Then there's Karl, remember? The gray German."

"Oh, yes, I know the gray German. He worked
With my old man. He had no teeth. No smile.
My mother always called him 'the Dutchman.'"

"Everyone in town called him the Dutchman.
He lived in that house you tell of over
By the swamp. That house with the ragg'ed flag
You'd see through his parlor window as you
Trudged from porches and kisses on your way
Home. Old Glory rose in the first world war,
When being a 'Dutchman' was a grim load
In a town with doughboys over there-ing
In France and mud. Karl raised the stars-and-stripes

In his parlor. But never in his heart.
Or so the town suspected. He kept it
Hanging there in his parlor on into
The next war. There it hung until he died
Dusty, ragg'ed, neglected, and ignored."
"Karl? Or the flag?"

"Both. But you know that."

"I know he worked with my old man and dug
Ditches. After work. And on Sundays, too."

"Yes, Karl dug ditches anyone needed."

"My old man said he enjoyed digging 'em.
As you or I love skating on a pond.
I never understood how that could be.
He said he loved staking a string from spike
To spike. And breaking the sod with a pick.
And tossing the dirt and earth and gravel
To a neat, brown mound beside the growing
Trench. Straight and neat and deep as a…as a…"

"Grave? Is that the trench you are looking for?'
"I never understood how a fella
Could love digging a ditch. It seemed so odd.
All that bending and swinging and sweating."

"Ha! That sounds like you on the baseball field.
Or your night hopes on a porch with a girl."

"So! *You* taunt *me*; but, I cannot taunt *you*?"

"No. No, you can't. Because I am a ghost.

And you are a boy with blood and blue thoughts
Who hears the click of pool balls and the groan
Of the wind, the song of a far guitar
And drums or a throbbing, distant organ."
And it is here that the boy interrupts.
"I love an organ at a carnival
But I hate an organ Sundays in church."

And why is Finch led to learn what he learns?
No person can remember everything.
Oh, people remember only little;
The poet notices and remembers
Most, nearly all, and he lives to remind
Mortal forgetters of maples and pines
And how a creek threads the green summer air
And how that air finds the breath of a boy
And the hair of a girl and draws the ear
Of a little brown dog to his hoping
A door will open. The creek threads the air
To lift the moon for a noticing boy
Who remembers life and love and kisses
Of the sparkle-eyed girl he so misses
And how it all tumbles in the speeding
Light automobiles streak upon the walls
And on the ceilings of village houses
Waking daylight as the night-love powders
All burned to a silver blue memory.
We tread upon our days and months and years
As if they were on-the-ground pine needles
Brown and quieted from life in the sun
And shade. This is what the poet recalls.
Annville starts at the bottom of a tree-
Tumble hill and flows green into dairy
Farms and woods gashed by a giggling creek.

Annville has tales and terrors and carries
A heft holy, hilly and heaped with leaves
And rattling atoms of every breathed breath
Of villagers and visitors alive
Or dying or dead. O! All those atoms
Like the frayed threads on the sleeves of a washed
And washed again fading denim work shirt.
And all those trees give leaf and limb to bird
And squirrel. They give shadow to the townsman,
Stories to the wind, etchings to the sky.
The sky gives back the magic of the moon
In a beam of light pooling on the trees
Silvering the leaves above ghost and Finch
And the grass beneath those two. How magic.
For the boy magic is all about books
And making room for glory or for grace.
Books, thoughts…good as a visit to a cave:
In, in, in you go as deep as you will.
And the danger—or the hope—the danger
Is you'll never come out, back to this world,
Atop the grass 'neath your feet. How magic.

Finch sighs, "Do we only live when we are
Believed into being? For God? Spirits?"

"There's the ag'ed thought, there's the ag'ed thought.
And thought asked is thought bubbled into words.
Into heard words, uttered trembling and brave."

"Will you say? Will you tell me? May I know?"

Alfred smiles at Finch. The smile draws dark lines
Across his cheeks, to his valley-deep eyes.
The ghost smiles at these questions. A gray grin.

Ahead of the sigh which always follows
Such questions. Such wonderings. Such eyed hopes.
Alfred smiles and holds Finch with those old eyes
The color of moss at night in cold spring.
"You know I won't, can't. And won't. How I'm here
And we can speak and hear is a ghost gift,
A mystery, a wrinkle, a wonder,
A chance. How is it that I was summoned?
Perhaps it was *you*, boy, who was summoned
To clear *my* thoughts, to summon *my* wisdom
To me. So that I can stop my gliding
And then zoom to some pleading, needing place
Or some soul lost in the coombe of despair
Like an old angel I once saw stumble
And fall and drop and bounce to icy earth,
Just a gust on the top of that night's snow
Feathering the diamond knoll up, up, up,
Into the numbed blue air. An old angel,"
Old Alfred muses, "tired, trembled, frozen
And failed." And he snaps around to the boy.
"And then there is love. Do you still know love?
That's all a ghost knows. Love and recalling.
I know you love. You long. You remember."

"*How* do you know?"

"I am a *ghost*."

"I want to be gone. I want to be here.
With her. I loved her so…long ago, found her
Again and glimpsed keys to unlock my now,
Do you know I own no month, none is mine?
Is this why I have longed to leave to find
A place, to find a time I wasn't strange

And could settle in and live in the sun
And dark, in the leaves, in the snow and wind?
I feel each month, each day odd and unowned
By me. I long to unlock my prison."
"Can you remember night, young Finch, can you?

"Such a question. Of course, of course, old ghost!"

"Ah, wait! I ask of night in a set time.
Night of a Friday. Or night of held hands.
Night with the air just ahead of a fog
That doesn't form; it lurks about unseen
To keep summer fevered even in the dark,
To keep eyes ahead though seeing, feeling,
Sensing, breathing, smelling, tasting who is
Beside you. Night that holds you just before
A sweet kiss. And that hope that hands will not
Let the other hand go, will not release."

Like a tavern Annville always tampered
With time. The tavern always turned the clock
Ahead, but the town caused the clock to fall
Behind and drag its people back with it.
Does Essie know the same dark enchantment
Of woods that Finch knows? Is that why she stays?
Or does she simply fear the world beyond?
It is here that we think of creeks. *That* creek.
Where it begins its tumble, its shudder
High on a hill above village and farm.
That granite hill and that tree-towered creek
Leaping, gurgling and bursting day and night.
It starts its tumble gasping in a spring
Somewhere high and hilly, to merge with snow
Losing its crystal to heat, to summer,

To the turning earth, the returning sun.
Down countless hillsides, down clefts and ravines
It flows, it tumbles, deepens and empties,
Always breaking into molecular
Mists in bowered woods, fine pieces of light
As if sprung from a far star or the eyes
Of a fox. And in a creek deep enough
For a boat or raft with a splashing oar.

This was how Alfred and Finch stopped meeting
And Finch escaped from Annville. This was how
A creek became a miracle passage,
A flowing, flying and watery flight
Along the lawns and left-behind longings
To burst, to blast, to tumble and fumble
Into the un-Annville air of a world
That Finch only dreamed to reach. Only dreamed.
And all we see in our emptying town
Is a ghost. A ghost graying. And staying.
This was to be how Finch hucked out of town.
He had walked the mossed banks beyond Annville.
He had seen the giddy cold creek grow and swell
With young summer, meeting and marrying
Other mad creeks eddying, advancing,
Roiling in noisy snakespeak on the way
To the Allegany and Ohio,
And continent-carving Mississippi.
Finch could never note the magic moment
When words flowed from trees—roots, branches, and leaves—
Into his pen and on to the thirsty
Page. That most magic moment summoning
The living, calling the dead to vivid,
Spinning, speaking, dancing sight in his mind,
In his eyes, in the flowing force of words.

How clouds above Annville and 'neath the sun
Swept their shadows over these holy hills;
Clouds over the village, under the moon
Invited the dead and drowsing shadows
Of the living to find blessed, mystic paths
Moist from roots, green breathing from leaves, from dark,
Forcing the branches to speak tales that tell
Of a town, of this town, of this Annville.

With his wispy head lowered, Alfred thinks
Of Finch walking away up Fair Oak Street.
"He's thinking of the creek, dreaming of wind
And how he has to free his mind and soul
From Annville. From the gin mills and the blood.
Free his mind and free his soul from Essie.
Thumb out o' town. In a truck. On a raft.
And he'll always hear that summoning creek.
He'll feel his ears burn with the cold. And he'll
See tail lights divide and dot the puddles."

It is here that Alfred pauses. Pauses
And watches Finch scuff away up Fair Oak,
Past a house sporting a trellis and moss
On the flagstone walk leading to the sagged
Porch. Seeing Finch leads to thoughts of himself.
And how it was he came to be a ghost.
In the recalled life whose chances were lost
To too many bars and too many shots
To the liver of a man in denim
Whose fraught face weathered from tanned to veiny.
And that sight within his head tumbles and stabs.
It is here that Alfred frowns and pauses
Watching. And he tries to swallow the thought
Rising in his throat. The thought is rising…

He is remembering. A staggering
Stumble at the end of the darkling lawns.
Alfred. Son. Father. And tippler, tumbler
Into the creek. There's a bottle smashing
On a streaming rock, bloodying Alfred's
Unyielding fingers. The creek, mist and dew
Seep with a thread of red. He had fallen
On many a morning. Sometimes in dark.
Sometimes in day. But those other mornings
The twitching sleep and writhing groans would give
To waking and aching and getting up.
Those mornings dimmed and blurred and were forgot.
That last morning of Alfred feeling shoe
On ground...was the last morning. The broken
Bottle and bleeding fingers were washed clean
In the juddering creek. They were washed clean,
Washed clean as the creek streamed into Alfred's
Lungs weighed with too, too many nights before.
The creek at the end of the lawns floated
Finch away. Like a walk along Fair Oak.
Like a door slammed shut on cursing and smoke.
Like a gate in a fence round a meadow.
The creek gave life to Finch. The creek wrested
Life from Alfred, washing blood from his hands
Filling his lungs with a black, weighted wet.
And turning him from spirits to spirit.

Beneath the Watching Hill

The town beneath the watching hill
has held our hearts three times.
I wait for you.
You walk to me.
We join for eggs and tea.
There is a pond
and butterflies.
Rain thrums the roof
above our kiss.
And my silly drive
up a hill, past flowers
big and white as popcorn balls,
stretches the day,
when you fear a storm
and need to be on your way.
A strange, forsaken little place
beneath the watching hill,
rather like the town
where I first saw you
and held your hand
under an umbrella.
And watched you ride
into the decades, away.
Did I say the place
beneath the watching hill
is forsaken? I mean to say
enchanted.

I Hate to Come in from a Storm

I hate to come in from a storm
Under the ruse of getting warm

While knowing well it's snowing well;
And in this snow I choose to dwell

(For just a while out in the cold,
I'm staying young, not growing old).

Hearing the wind groan and unfurl,
Out late, I worship the snow swirl.

Gone

I kneel at the edge of a pond.
Wind through the fronds
Pulses toward me and I feel
I'm on the deck of a boat asail
To a leafed and piney place where air
Is vapored and rustled with prayer.
I'm out for a final firefly,
Out before sleep at the end of day.
Elms lean over the rippling,
Juggling, bright, broken water.

Something Building

Across Fifty-sixth, behind a no-bill fence,
the muck is mapped by bootprints
and the ladder-rung tracks of a crane.
Brown puddles wobble the sun
and dirty it. A pile-driver drums
the day *prr-thonk, prr-thonk, prr-thonk.*
Belittled by rock mounds and snakey
rusted cables, workers in yellow helmets
survey and stamp and stoop.
All beards and plaid and hanging hair.
The mud-crusted boots, splattered pants
and cracked, brown hoods make them look
like Franciscans measuring
a path from breakfast to prayer.
Their heavy strides
keep time with the pounding. Taxis honk
and pigeons squawk
in the muddy middle of the lot
in the muddled middle of the city
where a building is rising, rising
from a rumour to a fact.
The workers trudge through the
gray light of spent night,
and in their considerations,
in the clutter of noise and spit
and steel, can *they* sense something building?

Antiverdant

There's a gravelly patch
north of Wakefield
where the Harlem line
opens up. Skinny trees sneak
about brick buildings
like a balding man's
precarious hair.
My nose burns from track ties
soaked to their soul in creosote.
I squint at the rails
(a rusty dust color like shame
at the thrown-away
New York *Suns*, Burma-Shave cans
and here a dead calico cat).
Blackened brick glooms my view
just north of Wakefield;
it wins the view and dims
the view; and stains
my sight with soot.

Rainfire

Night waves the train on,
Closer to the western mountains.
Rain starts soft and biblical,
Caught in its falling by a sun
Sad to set;
Sad to be done with play.
So it glows the rain to fire
And night waits.

East River

The gull in rosy
sunrise slices
with shadow
the houses
on Roosevelt Island.
The very air
is spirited,
drawing life,
drawing light
from the gull,
from the sun
and holds day halted,
not rising
nor falling,
unpeopled,
moving only
with the knifing gull.

North of Manhattan

The Hudson isn't a river;
it's a rumor. Fog creeps
over the water and hides
the chugging tugboat,
the car-dusty
bush and its berries,
and the wren nesting
on the bank. A wet wind
from the sea has conspired
a furtive fog and the Hudson
is only a rumor.

Misplaced

The house sits in colored city light
(Under rain falling from a brightened height)
As if dropped on its cement-locked block
By a vandalous wind, with a laugh.

This house is country (the lights are not)
Splintered and sagging on this littered lot.
The trees do well as city trees
Under lamps...from gas to neon.

But the house can't abide buses,
Five o'clock and its honking fusses,
Where the grass stops and the noise doesn't
And the dark is never fully dark.

New York to Chicago

Beside the west-bent train
farms all rocks and rot
keep up a brave, green front.
Trees bleed black into the fog.
The farms pass
and sink forgot
in the senile century.
A night's diesel-breath later,
the train huffs into the next city
and the track teeters high enough
to let me look into the sooty-building
bedrooms. Curtains wave out
the windows, but I don't answer;
I don't lift a hand.

What to Do with Light

The cold Egypt night is sinking
into the rippled sand
that later will warm my feet.
I squint my eyes
from the east side
of the morning hill.
The sun is come again
to cheer the rolling land,
glowing leaf and frond
with a small, poor gold.
I trudge here in the dark
before the tern is stirred
at the edge of the hills-away sea,
I trudge here before the desert rat
kills and eats,
and sleeps the day away.
I trudge
to my place beside the cave,
hugging this old robe
around my bone arms,
my feet slipping
in the frayed leather
of my sandals.
I trudge here in the dark
to my place beside the cave
and lay my rough sack
(with a loaf of yesterday's bread,
the flask of watered juice
and a looking glass) on the sand
waiting patient
for the sparkle of day.
My tongue urges my gums
to a toothless pink
and I squat and smile

at the worry
my bones will poke through
my flesh wrinkled brown
from heat and sand.
I trudge heavy-tired,
feeling my way
through denying night;
a sleep-wish weighs
just behind my eyes
until I squat
and smile
at the coming of the sun.
Women and men from far lands
will leave their jeeps
and scuff here,
where I squat and wait.
The women and men will bend
into this hole
in the hill and read
pictures scratched on the cold,
arid walls. Soon
I won't be alone
and I will raise my looking glass
to catch light and bend it
through the door of the cave,
like opening a book
pulled down from a high shelf,
pulled down from the dust
of time,
from the dust
of wind
and mystery,
holding hope
to be seen,

to be remembered
in the light
of my glass
bending the sun
into seeing.

Anymore

I don't splash
in the tree-leaning stream
or smell summer
in the air
and leaves dancing
over it
nor play baseball
nor steal beer
with Brogie
and Hamil
and Bob.
No wind
fingers my hair
as I fly my bike
through the air.
I don't dive into hay
in a cow-smelly barn
nor drink from that spring
in the firs
on the treed-and-mossed hill
above town.
No sleeping in a tent
whose canvas
splinters sunlight
into stars,
nor eating pieces
of dripping chicken
from a stick;
no kissing in the pines
behind the ballfield
nor stomping the road
as winter and the moon
keep stride.
I don't hide

nor seek
nor dam the creek
with sod stolen
from Ol' Buffin's pasture.
No rolling in oak leaves
nor sliding in snow
blued and soft and silent,
nor hunting wintergreen
in the sugarhouse woods
anymore.

More Than Music

I worship rain more than music
And it played all last night as I slept.
The applauding trees sounded
Like clouded sorrow,
Like a child begging
One more story,
One more catch,
A plea just ahead of bed.

I worship rain more than music
And it settled over the evening,
Conducting its sibilant aire
In the crowded sound summer composes:
Full of crickets and peepers and crows;
Full of yards-away dogs
And a nibbling deer
Closing the lid on the day.

Connecticut Testament

A hairy cloud harangues noon like a dark
prophet,
Spitting and raving of the storm to come.
Thunder shudders the ground before it's heard.
The scudding sky scowls and licks the green with
gray.
Annville cowers beneath the sky's contempt.
The leaves hush, grow still and wait. I squint
At the ripped, ripping cloud looming low.
Grass ripples like a shiver on my skin.
The cloud inks the oaks to silhouettes
Against a writhing sky, a deep seeping black;
Against some haughty hell from angry heaven.

Abandoned

There were no caves near home.
Dane and I vowed to dig one.
In the ninth-inning dusk
of a boy's unending summer
we vowed to dig a cave
in the pasture beyond
the barbed-wire fence.
So in the early sun
of the next day
(after our fathers were coffeed off
to work) we stole
two shovels and a pickaxe
and trudged through
thigh-high hay
dewing our pant-legs
and shoes.
Raising the top wire of the fence
with our scabby hands
we lowered the middle wire with a foot
and stumbled into the field
like convicts fleeing death row.
We found a mound
in the pasture (the cows
behaved as if it were visiting day),
we found a mound
and tossed hairy clods
up, up into the dusty air.
Our morning's work
carved a crater
in the mound
making more moon
than cave.
We left
without looking

into each other's face.
Back through the fence,
back through the grass
(dried of its dew) and
back through summer
hazing and sunning a field
sitting still
without a cave.

Swallows Still Visit the Barn

Grandfather, wind licks the leaves on the hills
Rising from the farm you farmed. But the pines
Along the long drive are gone. Remember
How they sighed in dusty summer when you
Took the milk to market? And how they wove
The groan of the snow slicking and drifting
And packing into heavy rest waiting
For sweet spring? And your hair-hooved work horses—
What were their names? Weren't they Hopple and
Chance?—
They're gone, too. They stood giant and gentle
Over you when you toppled from the stroke
That ended you and the farm. Remember
How always kind to those horses you were?
The feeding. The brushing. The few small loads
Of stones in the stone boat? And after work
You led them into the beloved clover?
The horses are gone, dear man. Remember
How you'd come in from morning chores and stoop
Down for a kiss on your whiskery cheek?
And grandmother'd serve heaps of homemade toast,
That morning's eggs, and spitting sausage you shaped
Evenings in your strong, red hands? Remember
The hay mow where I tumbled and I hid
While you milked the cows, shoveled steaming dung,
And pitch-forked down the silage and the hay
For those warm, long-lashed cows who you declared
Were pretty as movie stars? Remember
The rope I swung over the chaff-dust floor?
How I climbed up the wooden-rung ladder
Nailed to the wall? O swallows still visit
The barn, Grandfather, and red-winged blackbirds
Still flit and patrol the tangle-tongued creek.
But the hill-slope of corn is gone to moss.

Your Northern Spy orchard is down and done.
Now even clouds seem too hurried to pause
In the blue over the quieted pond
Where snakes played in the rocks. Some of your woods
Are mere stumps by the spring-frosted milk house
Turned shamed, graying foundation. Remember
That long two-path drive lined by pines blue-green
And dark? And snows have buried your story.
So others can't read it beneath the drifts,
Beneath ice, beneath life and forgot graves.
The years and light, shadows, and walks up hill,
Down pasture, the leaves of tolerant trees
The years have sewn their centuries like vines
Drooped with dew and days and dread. Remember
How you would fork the hay twice each summer
Onto the wagon and into the barn.
You'd cool the hot day with icy cider
Or frothed beer hidden with the tobacco
Grandmother forbid? Sunshine gave the air
A summery lust until night stirred birds
To peep to sleep you and the sighing cows.
Your canvas hat, your denim pants, your boots
With leather laces and a faded shirt
Waved windy threads from holes in the elbows,
The porch creaked and the dog dozed, remember?
Gone. Gone. All gone. As you, dear man, are gone.
As I am gone. And wishing you could know
Swallows still visit the barn, grandfather,
But, the hay stays in the field. And spiders,
I suppose, now rule over the hay mow.

Descrying

May I speak of a sight, of a vision
Showing young people, young village neighbors
Upon a frozen pond, frozen bright white
In a sunken village middle, all ringed
With trees and houses and gift-gold street lamps?

May I speak of the night of that vision
When, stepped from house warmth, I lean into night
With my ears and eyes tuned to December
While my mind shivers with the blest vision
Of them I knew, whom the years had stolen?

The moon is raked by clouds and by the wind
Bringing moaning word from the pulpit stars
On this winter night whose snow lifts silvered
As it listens to blue-chilled travel-tales
Of heaven and time and miles and missing

Them who stand upon ice down the dimmed years.
A wobbling night glowing a glow for wolves
Underneath bird-forsaken black branches
Whose seasoned sound now is the hymning wind,
The knowing wind, the blowing wind intent

On one more try at songs of things forgot
And dark and lived long ago and dearly
Singing of spirits, of shadows.   Or ghosts?
Faint, familiar faces of folks gathered
On pond ice; seen through gauze that softly smoothes

Their youth and hides laughing behind their eyes
Peering at some thing in the snow under
Their feet and all asparkle 'round their heads.
Is it Tartarus that frowns those frowned brows
'Neath the ice ringed by ignoring houses?

They are a group, but separate looking
At some smile-robber, at some thought-taker,
At some ice-wrinkle piercing passing life
That's chaining these spirits to this moment
From which flesh will mature, but leave the souls,

These so young souls, these never full-faded
Spectres that stand, hands gloved or pocketed,
Scarves dangling or tied over large, loose coats
From older sisters and armied brothers,
Wooled through many a winter, coats as much

Family as the beagle or grey cat
And holding cold in air and underfoot
Beyond their hearts and their heartened hopings
These youths of what-was, can—on a moaning,
Mooney night—gather, visit, and listen.

Need

Our moon was ours
Over rose and field
Between your door
And mine mere brief miles
Apart, away.

How was it we
Were diverted in
Child days laughing
All aglow at play
Apart, away?

Moving to meet
On a tree-sweet street,
A porch, a lake
Where the miles dissolved
And dropped away.

Beneath that moon
Our shyness, our eyes
Took in some thing
Grand upon the lake
Or in the leaves.

Oh, we have smiled,
Noting our friendship.
Friendship's easy.
It's love keeps us shy
Apart, away.

Friendship's easy.
It's love keeps us shy.
Latered in life
We need so to speak
Of what we feel.

The Church of Spring

Glowering clouds smother
The crystal haloed moon mother.
Clouds can't hold their night,
So they spill the hoarded dark.

The deep-throated wonder
That we've named thunder
Booms into a canticle
To spark sparkles

On the vestments of the pines
And wolves and rock shrines.
Bowing boughs and leaves drip
Into collection plates

We've named meadow and grass.
All this choiring, soaking mass
This hymning, psalming sobbing graces
Night and season and day…with worship.

A Weary Wait

There was moon enough
behind the clouds
to ghost the sky to glow.
Against the silver rent of rag
the maples and pines tossed
at two a.m. insomnia.
The wind waited up,
wanting company.
The needles and leaves
and a bat
and I
kept moving,
kept watch
until one could settle
on sleep.

Clarification

Each veined maple leaf is etched stark;
each shadow dies where light begins.
There's none of the sketching of haze.
A clarified air sharpens the day,
banishing dew, banishing fog.
Down the lane I see all I see beside me,
but small. Beech, a weeping willow
and ferns I could root in a jar on my window sill.
Tiger lilies and dandelions are dabbed
dots beneath blued clouds.
Fox and deer, take care.
This day things are easy
to see.

O, Allegheny

Leafed out on both sides, you thread
a wet smell into the Salamanca air.
Willows and oaks, along your banks, bow
over the current and see themselves
in the shuddering sun. You swirl beneath
Old Front Street Bridge, wide, arched iron,
bubbled rivets. I stop and lean on the scratched
cross-hatched railing to look down *on* you.
To look down *in* you. On every stroll
across the bridge I stop and look down.
Summer slows it all: you, sered river,
my thoughts, the buzzing day of heat,
of bugs, and you…so shallow
I see pebbles on the bottom.

Eavesdropping

Crickets chirr in the hazy air.
The needling spruce on the mossy shore

leans over the waves. Is it to catch
words hissed on the varnished boat?

The flailing-arm denials
of hating lovers? Does a possible gossip,

stir in the fir a hope of hearing more?
Does the blue tree lean in smug wonder?

Can it hear the hurts of the crying
woman in the red sweater hiding

her trembling chin? Does this evergreen
ever see the hair-mussed man rant

and shake his fist? After trying
to coax a fumbling, selfish love?

If a tree takes root, can a tree take note
of stabbing, cursing words wielded

by blood-tipped tongues? Two dwellers
on the planet, whose cooling heated hate?

Mid-August, Cape Cod

The shopkeeper scuffs out to her porch
and peers at the fog as if it were snow.
The bandbox behind the Chatham Inn
dulls empty, quiet in the settling night.
The sailor hears the Atlantic below the bluff.
The waves growl a late-day growl
that won't stop, won't vary until dark;
until dark and the fog weave
the air into a pact
to send the shopkeeper back inside,
to tie the sailor to the dock and
to bless the light beneath the street lamp
with useless gold.

An Emptying

Night is quicker to fall.
The temperature is quicker to fall.
Leaves and light, quicker to fall.
It's the falling of things,
an emptying –
of playgrounds
and ballparks
and lakes –
cooling the year.
Bright day is still summer,
still warm;
but, a chilled thread
woven of wind,
in the sun,
in the clouds,
and iron gray,
holds a secret we know
and pretend we don't.

A Tree and Time

Leaves on the birch flutter
in the autumn wind
and glint little glints
of the autumn sun
beneath the calm, pale sky
and a current-carried hawk
whose wings air their feathers
above the birch in the thrall of fall.
A maple and ash, a willow and beech
aren't moved by the wind.
They stand green and still and summer-y.
But the birch is giddy and golding
from the pulling fall
stirred to joy, though dying,
in the light and air
under a hawk-heaved sky.

Deliquescence

Let me be clear about fog.
I love it wispy,
strewn in the tops
of the summer woods
or twisting round the trunks
slow and white.
When it's left
by the leaving rain,
reaching, pleading for the cloud
that's meadows and counties away,
I love it.
I love it sad, abandoned,
on its way
to weaving grief,
dissolved, invisible
to the coming sun,
to the humming day.
Fog as shreds.
Hard to hold the eye
by its mourning,
morning fade.

Stitchwork

A bright, white gull flies
against a lumped bank
of wheezing-gray clouds.
She catches the sun
and flies with it
like a needle
sewing those clouds
to help them hold their rain.

Deciduous

Trees stoop.
Seeping October
(three days raining)
soaks the trunks black.
Late fall suffers
for its rude refusal to flee,
to die; it suffers with a litter
of thrown-down leaves.
They catch street lamps;
they craze light from a car
and brighten like a funeral cheek.
The leaves clump in the grass,
they lump out in the street,
tired by traffic tread, until
rain and rot write them
out of the world.

Catching Autumn

Down in a shadow, I look up
through the sunny umbrage;

through a trillion flaming
leaves, burning needy

and gaudy 'til they fall
from the effort. And the sky

has no more to do
but be blue.

Growing Late

The light can scarcely be called day.
Not sparkle nor glow, it's more gray

Like the weary work of a star
Filling in for some star afar

Taking leave, shirking his duty
Shunning the morning and beauty.

Neglecting august goldenrod,
Tiger lilies and sodden sod

Fall rains on this day in summer
A sad and bashful newcomer,

Wan hope for an invitation,
For gift this precipitation.

Quite cool enough to threaten frost
And like the sun, the season lost

To starlight dimmed and diminished
To summer, to morning, finished.

O, Church, Invite the Trees

O, church, invite the trees,
Invite the trees adorned with only leaves
And cones between the needles.

O, church, open your door
To squirrel and dog and deer,
Open your door to the wordless ones.

Pull back your ceiling
To the blue and sainted sky
And clouds and holy rain.

O, church, where are the stones?
And dust? Where are the tufts of hay?
A creek trilling down your aisle?

Forgive my sigh at the altar gold
And marble haloed men,
Mere men frozen, holding high hands

Their palms a blinding white
While your colored glass hides
The heaven of the world.

A Sense of Things

The opening door
pulls a line of air
across my face.
It turns me
from the window,
where I was thinking
of goldfinches and oaks.
I catch your eyes
just before I look away
and down.

Leaving

The track twinkles
A sent-ahead message
The local is coming.
Church bells from off
Methodist way
Wrinkle Sunday.
The insects of afternoon
Are humming.
I climb on the Sabbath train
To ride to a place called work.
And in my head
Regret is drumming.

O, Snow

What have you done
to send the neighbors south?
Line the limbs
with soft hoar
and pile flecks to sparkle
and give shadows a blue glow?
O, snow...what have you done?

Candle in a Window

Cradled in a cloud, the floating moon
sifts light down on December,

softening the tin-brittle air. Icy stars
poke the sooted sky and try to lure

pines behind the hill house to reach, reach
and lose. A candle in the window tries

to keep Christmas: a hazy flame, a timid
try for brightness, failing, fading. A dulled

spirit unable to shine out on the snow
or back in the room. It flickers, falls short,

falls faint; not-quite day,
not-quite night, not-quite light.

At Fall of Night

At fall of night
Frogs peep in the air.
While goldenrod powders the wind
Sun loses hold on the green.

At fall of night
Birds string their settling air
From hay-sewn nest to far-flown kin.
Stars spin out to be seen.

And in the night
If a walker should dare
To attract night's notice to him,
Night ought never to be mean.
The night ought to be keen
And honor long a walker's whim:
To walk in dark, to dare,
At fall of night.

Islands of the Night

In the tangle of time
Through bare branches,
Clouds lie
In the black sky
Stretched and thinned
By the wind.
The clouds part
From the moon; then,
Cover the moon,
Taking the moongift glow
Ragg'ed continents show.
Port of ghosts,
Harbored rememberings.
Longing of belonging
On the sparkle and ice
In the black sky,
These mapped only tonight
Islands streak like a fox,
Like a sung song,
Like a kiss in the pines,
Pulled to wavy, hazy gauze.
Who peoples those clouds?
Ragg'ed farmers
And factory hands?
Wives who fell through love
To death and drink?
Sons shivering hope
Out of their hearts
And daughters who put down
More than dolls?
On the ragg'ed islands
Mapped on this night
Do names turn to curses?
Or do they polish

In the vapored wind
And join the sparkle
Of stars?
Clouds lie
In the black sky,
Ragg'ed, bright,
Mapped only tonight.
They dim the moon,
Its middle-night threads
Of fabric islands,
Of unreachable beaches
Of hills that surround
Valleys one moment,
Then sink to become them
The next.

December Fifth

It's snowing.
In the blued twilight
of near winter
it's snowing.
Townfolk are heading
into church,
hands stuffed
in coat pockets.
Collars pulled up
over their ears.
Breaths feather, too,
into the blue
of leaving day.
I could join the faithful
and leave the cold,
leave this cloud-cluttered
hour and slip
into church with them.
But, it's snowing.
That is what *I* worship.
And in the morning
frost will flower the sidewalk.

Aftermath

Two days after the blizzard
I crunch on stucco snow,
packed on the roofs,
packed on the lawns,
pulling air down in blue
shadows. Oak limbs spread
against the china sky;
twigs poke from the drifts.
The winded ridges
and the rubble of the plows
burn day to more day
than winter allows;
a battle won in a lost war.
The already dead
cannot die more.
And the sun works twice:
in blinding white light;
and by laying shades
across March and me
of all that outlives winter
and all that will glow
when the snow is gone.

Age

He lies on his mussed bed
reading. Damn. As if
the smudged, scratched glasses,
weren't enough, his eyes reflect
in the lenses. Wrinkles
sluice across his lids
and cheeks, in the prescribed
mirror. They look like
the plowing around
elderly eyes.
Age snaps through him
smelling of acrid air
and defecting hair.
Age groans in his head
as he lies reading on his bed.
Elbow aches; dandruff flakes;
sneaky age snakes
through him
like browned grass
on the baseball field
limped to autumn, mitts away.
He feels dust seeping
into his soul.

Old Randolph Road

It could lump-run straight
but not for long.
Rambling blacktop
with a hay field off right
and from the left
trees stooping
for the wind
of the speeding auto.
Do they wish
they could thumb a ride
and pass through land,
pass through time?
The road's dirt was
coffined
in concrete; and that
was waked to blacktop.
Gnarling, bending
crashes testify
blood doesn't hurt
but winter will take
the highest hope,
crack it, pock it
and show the road
it has no business
invading, slicing a field.
Not like
an upended ancestor
consigned to a creek-bed:
A surreal city
of jagged concrete gravel
and twisting steel cables,
with the mailbox names
of snakes who live there,
lurk there in a city

of discarded, jagged road
dumped by the creek.
It carried me
nowhere,
but now in
dreams
it bums me back.
All the sights
of the seasons
shelve snugly
in thoughts.
All the sights
to come
on the grumbling gravel road,
all the sights
to come.

Tangible Time

Some times in Annville
everything is gray:
gray streets, gray walks,
gray walls, gray sky.
And one gray afternoon,
gray men in a library
sit and lean against
backdrop books.
The colored spines
border the men, but
don't touch them,
their eyes
like emptied creek bank
homes of terns flown
away to warmth.
The eyes glisten over
gaping smiles.
They flutter like a spark
trying to ignite.
And gray settles
as dust in a rut.
The men seem dropped,
waiting to be plucked.
In the hard current
of years they're swept
to a stagnant pool, a wasting,
waiting, crumbling moment.
Under an unseen marker
of what should have been
and isn't.

Looking After

The wind leaned the maple
over my reading
and dusk sipped the words
into what the dusk became:
night.
Ink is a gift:
it unwraps a laying-down sun,
gives a bird a song
and gives shivers to the rain.
As that dusk gave all
to night
and my book sighed to unseen,
there were only fireflies
with their brief, green ease
to show me in the dark
how to find home.

Connecticut Psalm

Let my sleep be just enough.
Let my sleep clarify the day
And give it open-eyed noticing.
Let leaves, against gray and sinking clouds,
Let leaves toss in the giddy wind.
And let that wind flutter the fur
Of the fox, of the dog.
Let the fox be caved and safe,
Let the dog click home along the berm,
Scents and sounds enlarging
Within his small and sacred brain.
Let grass ripple, let grass ripple
And let stars spin silver-pricked and far.
Let the pond shudder.
Let the lilies bend.
Let the clarified day show all there is
To worship. And let it show me
One sweet gift
It has never shown before.

Asking God

Do you demand praise?
I suppose you do from some psalm.
But the man as flesh as I
orders me to praise you.
And I do. In his words.
Not mine. In his church.
Not mine. I hear the trees
susurrating nights and days
in the wolf-wise wind,
gathering soul dust
on its never resting rounds.
That is where I hear praise
or wish to offer it:
to the wind, to the trees,
to the roiling clouds
living twice: in the orbiting sky
and the juddering pond.
Praise as mystery, as secret,
offered as hope, not fact.
Will you accept that praise?
Will you look upon me
in patience, in knowing
I am finished with asking?
I am working on accepting.
Your distance. My place
under trees, in clover breeze
juggling light like laughter.

Closing Time

Last one in the restaurant,
my elbows dig in the crumbs

on the checkered tablecloth.
My coffee's cooled to warm.

Pots sing from suds
out in the kitchen sink.

I dare not look up
for a hot refill.

I dare not wink or wave
Or sigh. I simply sit

and read page four
of the *Annville Hub* a third time.

I sip away without complaint
for fear I'll see the weary dark

beneath the waiter's eyes.
And ask him for my check.

Elegy

Clouds dome the morning.
Last night's storm—
lightning next door,
cackling, stabbing thunder,
a wall of straight rain—
has left this new day
cold, grayed and weary.
Perhaps even dead.
And the August leaves
with leaving green
are flowers
about to fall
on summer's grave.

About the Author

Ira Joe Fisher's poetry has appeared in *Poetry New York, The Alembic, The New York Quarterly, Entelechy International, Diner, Ridgefield Magazine, The New Hampshire Review* and the anthology *Confrontation.* He is the author of *Some Holy Weight in the Village Air* and *Songs From an Earlier Century* as well as *Remembering Rew,* a chapbook. Ira has a Master of Fine Arts degree in poetry from New England College. He has taught poetry, communications, and broadcast history there. He teaches poetry and creative writing at the University of Connecticut and Mercy College in Dobbs Ferry, New York.

Ira regularly performed in the long-running musical *The Fantasticks* in the 1990s and productions at New York City's Lambs Theatre and the reader's theatre drama *The Garden of Dromore* presented at the New York University Hot Ink Festival. Ira appeared in the film *California Girls, Try to Remember: the Fantasticks,* and in the ABC daytime drama "Loving" and—for ten years—on the CBS *Early Show.* Ira and his wife, Shelly, have four children. He and Shelly live in Connecticut with their Welsh Corgi, Lily.